ANIMAL
RECORDS

First edition for the United States, Canada,
and the Philippines published 1992
by Barron's Educational Series, Inc.

© Copyright by Aladdin Books, Ltd 1992

Design David West Children's Book Design
Illustrations Kate Taylor
Text Anita Ganeri
Picture research Emma Krikler

Created and designed by
N.W. Books
28 Percy Street
London W1P 9FF

All inquiries should be addressed to:
Barron's Educational Series, Inc.
250 Wireless Boulevard
Hauppauge, NY 11788

International Standard Book No. 0-8120-6300-7

Library of Congress Catalog Card No. 91-31321

Library of Congress Cataloging-in-Publication Data

Ganeri, Anita 1961-
Animal records / by Anita Ganeri : illustrated by Kate Taylor--1st ed.
p.   cm -- (Animal questions and answers) Summary: Introduces,
in question and answer format, record-breaking animals, including
the biggest, smallest, shortest, and tallest creatures on earth.
ISBN 0-8120-6300-7
1. Animals -- Miscellanea--Juvenile literature. (1. Animals-
-- Miscellanea. 2. Questions and answers.) I. Taylor,
Kate, ill. II. Title. III. Series.
QL49.G242   1992
591 -- dc20   91-31321   CIP   AC

Printed in Belgium

2345   0987654321

QUESTIONS AND ANSWERS ABOUT

ANIMAL RECORDS

Barron's

Which animals are record breakers?

Animal record breakers come in an amazing range of shapes and sizes. They include huge elephants and tiny spiders no bigger than a dot. Some are very tall. Some are very short. Some speed along. Others move very, very slowly. This book will help you learn more about the biggest, smallest, shortest, and tallest animals on Earth.

Which animal is faster than an express train?

The peregrine falcon can move faster than any other creature on earth. It flies high up in the air, looking for small birds to catch and eat. Then it dives down on its prey at amazing speeds of up to 80 miles (130 kilometers) an hour. This is faster than an express train.

Which is the slowest animal?

Snails move very slowly indeed. It would take a snail 33 hours to walk one mile on the ground (about 1½ kilometers). You could do it in about 20 minutes!

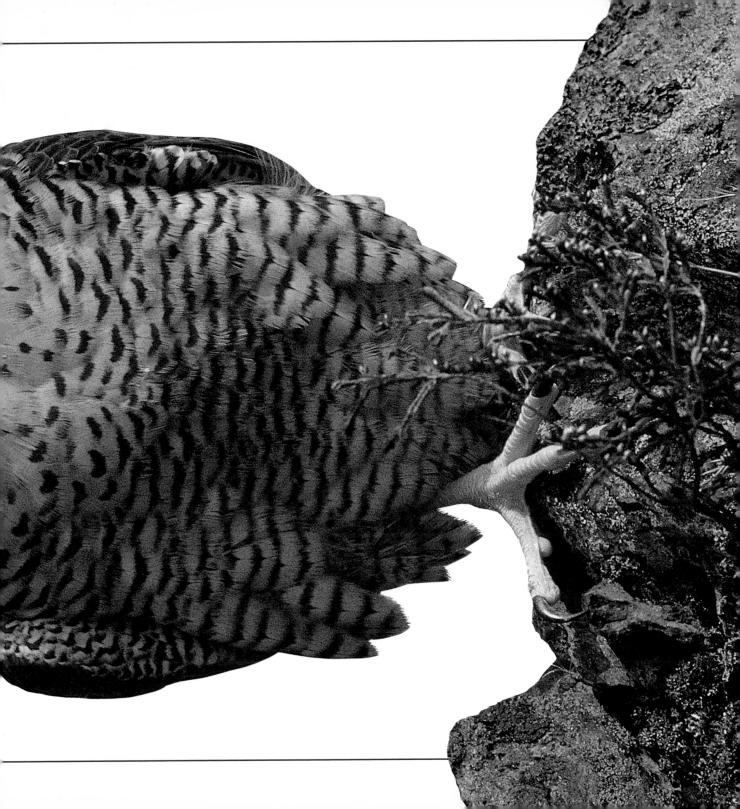

Which animal has the longest neck?

Giraffes have the longest necks of all. They also have very long legs and so they are the tallest animals in the world. They can stand over 6 yards (nearly 6 meters) high. Even newborn giraffes are 2 yards (nearly 2 meters) high – as tall as a very tall human.

Which antelope has legs thinner than pencils?

Royal antelopes are only the size of large hares. They are the smallest antelopes on earth. A small royal antelope has legs thinner than pencils. It could easily stand in the palm of your hand.

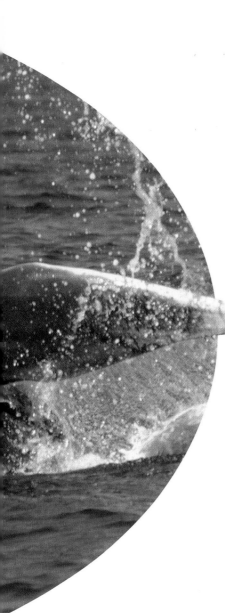

Which is the largest animal that has ever lived?

The gigantic blue whale can grow to be 108 feet (33 meters) long – longer than a tennis court. It can weigh as much as 20 elephants. A blue whale's tongue alone can weigh an amazing four tons.

Which mammals weigh less than Ping-Pong balls?

The world's two smallest mammals are the pygmy shrew and the bumblebee bat. Even the adults weigh less than Ping-Pong balls.

13

Which bird lays eggs as big as melons?

The ostrich is the biggest bird on earth and lays the biggest eggs. One ostrich egg is about as big as 24 hens' eggs. It would take about 2 hours to boil and could feed 12 people. The eggshell is thick and strong. You could stand on it.

Which bird is only as long as your thumb?

Bee hummingbirds are tiny. They are less than 2½ inches (64 millimeters) long and are lighter than some moths. Their bills and tails make up half their length.

Which animal has the longest hair?

The musk-ox lives in the Arctic where it is freezing cold and icy. It has very thick hair to keep it warm. Its hair is also longer than that of any other animal. It can grow up to 35 inches (90 centimeters).

Which animal has the longest antlers?

The moose has antlers which measure 6 feet (nearly 2 meters) across. The moose grows new antlers each year.

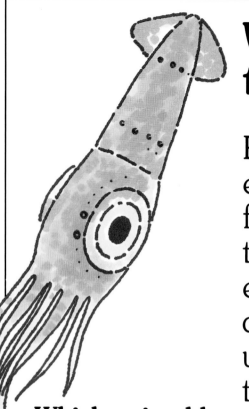

Which animals have the best eyesight?

Birds of prey have superb eyesight for spotting their prey from high in the air. Eagles have the best eyesight of all. Their eyes are about the same size as ours, but they can see up to eight times further than we can.

Which animal has eyes that are bigger than a long-playing record?
The giant squid has bigger eyes than any other animal. Its eyes are nearly 17 times wider than our eyes, and bigger than a long-playing record.

19

Which animals have the shortest lives?

Many insects have very short adult lives. Male houseflies live for only 17 days. Some mayflies live for only a few hours as adult insects. This is just long enough to find a mate and lay eggs.

20

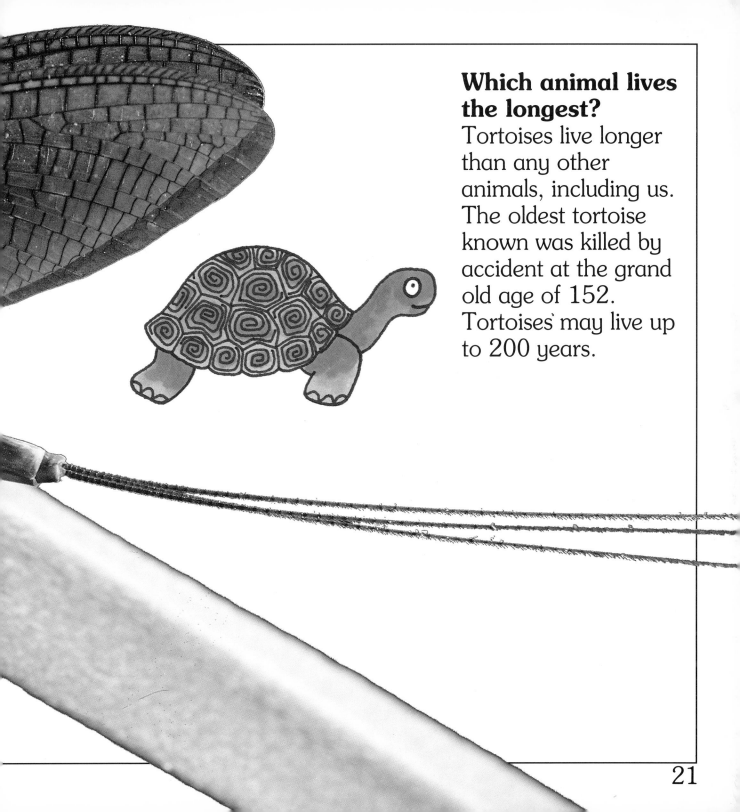

Which animal lives the longest?

Tortoises live longer than any other animals, including us. The oldest tortoise known was killed by accident at the grand old age of 152. Tortoises' may live up to 200 years.

Which bird flies furthest?

Each year the Arctic tern flies from the Arctic to the Antarctic and back again. This is a round trip of almost 25,000 miles (40,000 kilometers). It is the longest journey made by any animal. In its lifetime, a tern flies the same distance as a trip to the moon and back. It spends eight months of the year flying.

Which bird stays in the air the longest?

The common swift leaves its nest, then spends two to three years in the air. It eats, drinks, and even sleeps in the air. It does not land until it is old enough to breed.

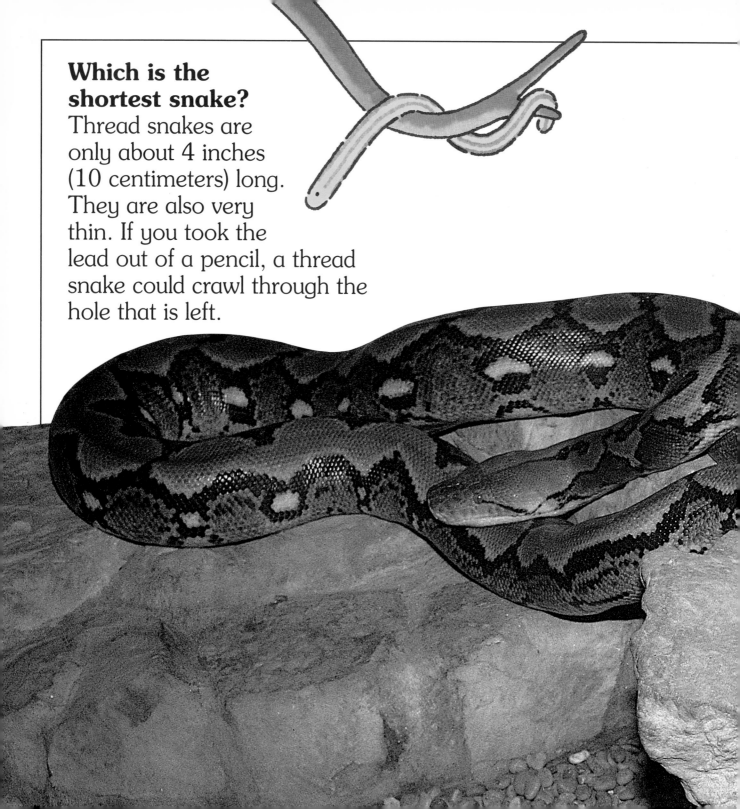

Which is the shortest snake?

Thread snakes are only about 4 inches (10 centimeters) long. They are also very thin. If you took the lead out of a pencil, a thread snake could crawl through the hole that is left.

Which snake is nearly as long as three cars?

The longest snake on earth is the reticulated python. It can grow up to 32 feet (about 10 meters) long, nearly as long as three cars. The anaconda is not quite as long as the python, but it is much heavier. Both snakes squeeze their prey to death.

Which snake has the longest fangs?

Gaboon vipers have fangs as long as your little finger. They are the longest fangs of any snakes. The vipers use them to stab their prey and inject it with poison. When they are not being used, the fangs are folded back inside the viper's mouth.

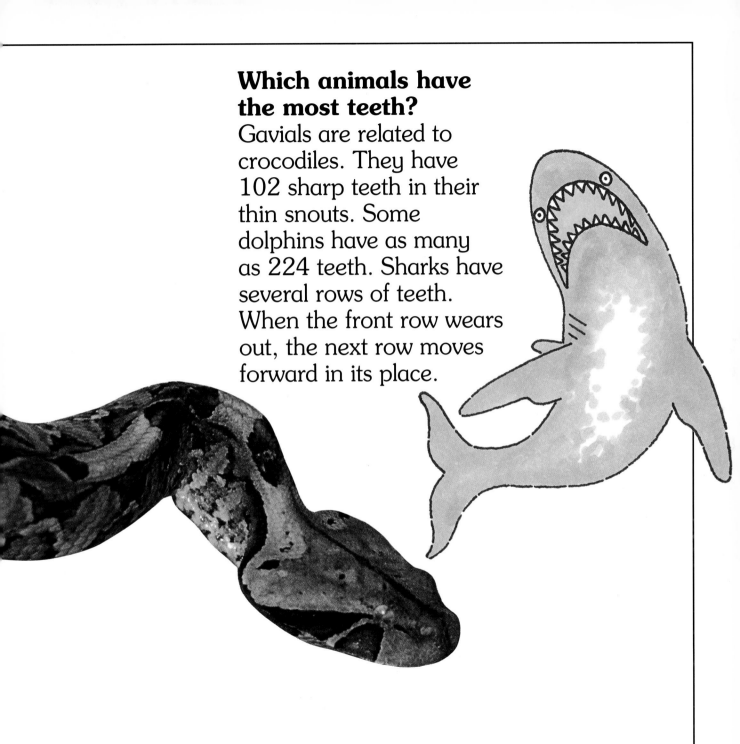

Which animals have the most teeth?

Gavials are related to crocodiles. They have 102 sharp teeth in their thin snouts. Some dolphins have as many as 224 teeth. Sharks have several rows of teeth. When the front row wears out, the next row moves forward in its place.

Which spider has the longest legs?

Huge tropical bird-eating spiders measure over 11 inches (27 centimeters) across their outstretched legs. They have long fangs and hairy bodies. They don't use webs, but pounce on birds and small creatures.

Which is the biggest shellfish?

The giant clam's shell is over 1 yard (about a meter) wide. The shell's edges are like a saw. They fit together tightly enough to hold a thin piece of wire.

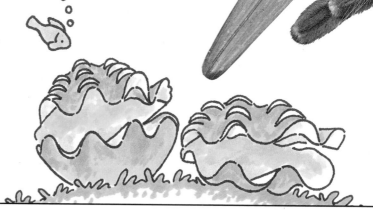